STORYTELLING

SECRETS

FOR SUCCESSFUL SPEECHES

Mark Davis

**Melbourne Education & TrainingCentre
Australia**

Ph: +61-404-178-126
Email mark@mastertheartofpublicspeaking.com

Also by Mark Davis:

Public Speaking Magic
How To End Our Speech With Confidence
Excite, Engage, Entertain

STORYTELLING
SECRETS
for SUCCESSFUL SPEECHES

7 strategies for
telling stories
people love

Mark Davis

Table of Contents

Foreword

What is the secret to delivering powerful and persuasive presentations? Stories.

Well-crafted and presented stories help get our message across without sounding like we are preaching. Stories are the "Trojan Horse" that sell the message and the idea, while packaged in the form of entertainment.

When the audience feels like we are sharing with them instead of preaching to them, it makes it easier for them to accept the message.

The best secret I ever learned as a coach was to help people see themselves in the stories of others. To see the highs and lows. And to see the potential they have for transformational change.

Their habits, their attitude, and even their thoughts are easier to influence with a good story. They get the lesson and feel like they taught themselves.

I have been looking forward to some fresh ideas on storytelling … and this book delivered!

I have a new resource now to help create stories for my presentations and coaching sessions.

Flick to any section of this book for inspiration to create stories, or turn your existing stories into something awesome.

From now on, you will be a Master Storyteller, and public speaking will be easy.

To your story!

Akash Karia
Storytelling strategist and bestselling author of *How to Deliver a Great TED Talk.*
AkashKaria.com

Storytelling Secrets

Storytelling secrets are strategic ways to create stories we can retell for maximum impact.

This book isn't going to cover the entire subject of public speaking; it will focus on helping you become better at creating and telling stories.

The seven secrets are:

- Secret stories – "Curiosity and irresistibility"
- Funny stories – "Telling it with humor and making it memorable"
- Past and present stories – "When I was Young"
- Other people's stories – "Personal stories and the stories of others"
- Emotional stories – "Create an emotional response"
- Before and after stories – "Transformation"
- Sales stories – "Testimonials, referrals, reviews, and the power of the third party"

Get notified when the next new public speaking book is released by subscribing at the website:
http://www.mastertheartofpublicspeaking.com

Find the schedule of live events including seminars, workshops, webinars and coaching programs at
http://www.markdavis.com.au

If you would like a public speaking workshop in your city, or for your group, contact Coach Mark Davis directly at Mark@MasterTheArtOfPublicSpeaking.com

Secret Stories

"Can I tell you a secret?"

Who can resist?

Any story that begins with this opening will grab the audience's attention.

This is what we want.

A few examples

"Can I tell you a secret? Over the last few weeks, I've been thinking about quitting smoking. I just lost another family member to lung cancer, so I have no more excuses. Can you help me quit?"

"Can I tell you a secret? I think the world is dangerous. When I was a kid, I would ride my bike around town until eight pm. I rode the bus alone and wouldn't think twice about it. Today, we're not even safe in our own homes. This is why I have a security system."

"Can I tell you a secret? When I was a teenager, I had a weight problem. I couldn't put on weight. It didn't matter what I did, I was a bag of bones. Finally, I got the nutritional and psychological support I needed to eat properly and keep the weight on, so now I look healthy and have more energy."

Secrets are the perfect story starters

- People find secrets irresistible
- People will lean in to listen to a secret
- People love the privilege of being told a secret
- People love to be the first to hear a secret
- People will stop everything else they are doing to hear a secret
- Secrets hold special value higher than news and current affairs
- People love to gossip

Secrets about our own lives are personal and powerful, and secrets about other people are considered "gossip," which is more powerful for grabbing attention.

Yes, secrets are juicy and delicious.

Sharing a "secret" story about someone else

"Let me tell you a secret. I learned this from my uncle, who runs a music shop. He said, that if we want to get ahead, we have to work multiple jobs while we're are young and have lots of energy, before we have a family and other responsibilities. He used to work a regular eight-hour day, and then work three hours tuning pianos. Doing this, he created a multi-million dollar business."

"Let me tell you a secret. Mandy has not always been that skinny. Once upon a time, she weighed over two hundred pounds! Do you know how she lost all that weight?"

"Let me tell you a secret. That guy over there, Tim, is a multi-millionaire. You know how he did it? He became an rideshare driver in the first weeks the company launched, and as a pioneer, he got a great reputation for service and quality. He was asked to speak about it, be the face of the company. Now, he travels the world as a motivational speaker, talking about ridesharing."

"Let me tell you a secret. I never used to be this popular. I took confidence classes and trained in public speaking training. I read a lot of books and I learned how to talk to people, discovering different personality styles, to become a communications expert in two years. Now, I train people around the world."

Permission

Giving and getting permission to listen to a secret calms people, so they do not have to feel so strange about hearing a secret. They'll listen even more intently, because the secret includes a surprise.

Permission is a polite way to get the audience to agree to be told a secret.

"Can I tell you a secret?"

"Is it okay if I tell you a secret?"

"Would it be okay to share this secret of success with you?"

"When I heard this weight loss secret, I knew you'd would want to know. Can I share it with you?"

"When I heard of this secret skincare ingredient, I had to tell you. Can you guess what it is?"

I do not think anyone would refuse to hear a secret, since it is human nature to want to know. Curiosity kills the cat, because it can't resist.

Hearing a secret is like getting an unexpected gift, a free bonus when you buy something at full price, and the surprise makes us feel good.

The element of surprise

A secret should take people by surprise and it may even take their breath away. It should be something almost scandalous, with controversy, revelations, and drama. This melodrama around its "revelation" is pure theatre.

Things to avoid in telling our secret stories

- Simple facts—people can guess these on their own, so there needs to be more background.
- Someone else's story—it must be original.
- Being too long-winded—short secrets are more dramatic; more shock value is in a quickly told story.
- Strangers—we consider celebrities people we know.

When we get people to stop what they're doing, to pay attention to a story, it has to be worth it.

Secrets give people something new.
Secrets let us inside the private world of famous people.
Secrets are perfect sound bites to share with others.

All because they provide shock, surprise, and a change in our day, and give us something new to talk about.

Once someone knows a secret, they want to be the first to tell someone else while it is still new.

When a speaker shares a "secret" story, we sit in the audience and assume they have never told anyone before; therefore, it will be special, because it is new and the story will be fascinating because it will be outrageous or controversial.

What is another way to open this type of story?

- I have never shared this before
- I have never shared this with a big group
- I have never shared this outside of my company
- I have never felt comfortable sharing this
- I have not told this story outside of Australia

More about secrets

Secrets are powerful tools when they are about a successful person, or a celebrity, or someone in the public eye. And the more details we share, the more exclusive the secret story feels, and the people hearing it feel lucky, even inclusive.

Television infomercials thrive on telling stories to create sales. This is why they use celebrities, singers, movie stars, and actors.

In the movie, Joy, featuring Jennifer Lawrence, we saw this principle at work. Her personal stories about creating the self-wringing mop started a revolution in TV home shopping. Just a few years later, she had a billion-dollar business on QVC and later on the Home Shopping Network.

With the secret of the self-wringing mop, she revolutionized not just cleaning, but how people sell products on TV.

What are some of the ways we can share just one secret?

- This weight loss secret is just for those of you who came here today.
- This modem secret will revolutionize how you use the internet.

- This lighting secret will change the way you make videos.
- This productivity secret will save you two hours a day.
- This algorithm secret will help you spot the best stocks to invest in.
- This automotive jargon secret will give you the inside track on the best car to buy.
- This engineering secret will explain why China is taking over the world.
- This frequent flyer secret will debunk every myth you've heard about traveling in Asia.
- This pheromone secret will give you the magic touch with women.
- This posture secret will help gain you more confidence around men.
- This wrinkle-removing secret ingredient will give you younger looking skin in just two minutes a day.
- This eye contact secret will help you deliver powerful presentations.
- This amino acid secret ingredient will make your energy levels skyrocket.

Now, let us add an object to our magic words to see how they make our story more compelling:

- This secret ingredient…
- This secret Facebook trick…
- This secret photography tip…
- This secret system…
- This secret connection…
- This secret activewear fabric component…
- This secret lasagna preparation method…

- This secret shaving tip…
- This secret investing strategy…
- This secret antioxidant…
- This secret energy pill…
- This secret skincare routine…
- This secret face mask ingredient…
- This secret fat-burning exercise…
- This secret power phrase…
- This secret sequence of words…

Secrets are compelling to listen to.

What are some more good storytelling openings?

Magic

Magic is mystical and wonderful. While people may not totally believe in magical tricks, illusions, and sleights of hand, they do want to believe amazing things can and will happen. And when they do happen, it is like magic, so we all become childlike in the presence of magic and magical things.

This is why "magic" is a great word to use in our story opening.

- "I am going to share with you the magical secret of the Dead Sea Salts."
- "I am going to share with you the three magical words that will get any woman to fall in love with you."
- "I am going to share with you the magical secret world of celebrity fitness trainer, Mr X."
- "I am going to share with you the magic skincare secrets of this famous movie actress."

- "I would like to tell you about the magic ingredient in this bottle of super vitamins."
- "I would like to share with you the magic numbers that have unlocked the key to my success in investing."
- "I would like to give you the magical secret sentence used by professional salespeople to get higher value sales."
- "I would like to give you the magical secret interview technique by successful entrepreneurs to attract good staff."
- "I have to give you this secret: it is magical, and it will change your life."
- "I cannot believe this magical secret has remained hidden for so long. Here, now, is the key to eternal youth."
- " I cannot believe this magical secret has been hiding right in front of our eyes: the key to long-lasting energy."

If we use the word "magic," we can watch the audience's eyes light up because of the element of surprise. Surprise feels good. And that is another keyword we can use.

Surprise

"I have a surprise for you today."

Every audience loves a surprise, especially when they have trust in the speaker, or the salesperson, or the lecturer, or the CEO up on stage.

Surprises tap into our childhood because most surprises were positive, with events like Christmas and birthdays, visits from our friends and family, grandmothers arriving out of the blue, brothers flying back from overseas.

Sand from the Sahara
Silk scarves from Thailand
Smoked salmon from Alaska

All of these gifts are unexpected—surprises. And they have a positive effect on our feelings and emotions.

So let's use "surprise" in a series of story openings.

- "I have a surprise for you today: not one, but two great stories of success with this product."
- "I have a surprise for you today: not one, but five guest speakers to share their stories about how to be successful."
- "I have a surprise for you today: the most successful trader in the company is here to tell his story. From today onwards, it will be easier for you to make money."
- "I have a surprise for you today, and it is attached to someone's seat. Please reach under to see if anything is stuck to your chair. If so, you have won a five-night vacation to the Bahamas."
- "I have a surprise for you tonight: your ticket has been entered into a lucky draw and someone will win $99 worth of skincare just for showing up."
- "I have a surprise for you tonight: the story I am about to tell you goes back over four thousand years, handed down from generation to generation, from father to son. And now, I will share it with you."
- "I have a surprise for you tonight: the story I am about to share is incredible, and you are the first people in the country to ever hear it."
- "I have a surprise for you tonight: the people in the front row will become actors in the story I am about to tell."

- "I have a surprise for you tonight: the story I just told was true, and it was my story."

Just like with magic, people love surprises. When something unexpected sneaks up on us, we feel a thrill, and this is a positive emotion that releases serotonin, which makes us happy and relaxed.

After the thrill is gone, though, we have an audience ready to listen, so we must make the stories in our surprises count.

Announcements

Stories can also use the announcement method, which tells the audience we are about to share something interesting or important.

- "Ladies and gentlemen, I have an announcement to make: this next story is top secret, and I'd like you all to pay attention as I can only share it once."
- "Ladies and gentlemen, I have an announcement to make: the secret you've all been waiting for is on this table under this sheet. I am about to reveal it, but first, let me tell you a little about it."
- "Ladies and gentlemen, I have an announcement to make: the story you're about to hear deals in ghosts, extraterrestrials, conspiracies, and more. So strap yourself in, it is going to be a wild ride."
- "Ladies and gentlemen, I have an announcement to make: tonight's story begins in a town just like this, in a room just like this, with people who looked just like you do. Let's begin."

Storytelling Secrets
for Successful Speeches

When I was young, I had to work two jobs through the summer to pay for university. At night, I played piano at the local hotel, and during the day, I worked on farms, helping to bring in thousands of bales of hay.

Why did I do this? Because I wanted to buy an electric piano. I wanted to travel. And I wanted to be independent.

Every story needs to have a purpose that makes it relevant and relatable. If we unlock some strategic ways to start a story, then we will have a treasure chest of material when we talk.

Most people have the attention span of a goldfish. If we are boring for more than seven seconds, we will lose our audience to their phones, their imaginations, or to the person beside them.

This is why we opened with the storytelling secret opening #1: - "Can I tell you a secret?" With an interesting first chapter like this one, the reader is pulled into the book.

When we see our audience isn't paying full attention, what do we do?

Give some amazing statistics?
Try to be funny?
Speak louder?

Relax. The secret is to tell a story in using one of the seven methods described here. Only storytelling guarantees we will hook the attention of the audience, and they'll be engaged in what we have to say.

The goal, however, is to be more than just interesting. It is being the most engaging and relevant for our audience, and stories connect with the program in our head that says "pay attention."

We can link stories to our key points.

We can tell stories that teach a lesson.

We can create stories to give context and meaning to our message.

We can retell good stories again and again; they'll stay relevant and interesting.

It helps to have a systematic approach, a storytelling strategy, and know how. Instructing people to "just tell stories" is like saying to a comedian "just be funny."

Relevance

Have a story and link it to your message.

If we want to make a point about leadership, then we need a story that demonstrates that personality trait or action.

Need to make a point about persistence? Refer to a great achievement in history that took a while to accomplish—sieges, battles, discoveries.

Maybe we would like to have the audience feel an emotion? Then we need to immerse them in a personal story.

Every story has to begin and follow a theme or a style.

If we learn to tell different stories, then we can choose one appropriate for our talk. If we practice telling these stories during our preparation time, then we can easily retell them during our speech without referring to notes.

We can have a complete toolbox of interesting stories to tell.

Want an example?

The first big concert I went to was U2, Rattle and Hum in 1989, with BB King and his band as the opening act. It was a great live experience of music I had only heard on CDs up until then.

Additionally, it was a unique, moving, and connecting experience, and when I listen to their music today, I remember that live event as a highlight of my youth. The music, the energy, the emotion—it was all unforgettable.

Now, whenever possible, I make it a point of seeing anyone I like, "Live." These performances bring the studio recordings to life and make them more valuable.

A story, with a relevant point.

The Storyteller

For thousands of years, the storyteller was the key person in the tribe. All of the tribe's history, the group, and the race was passed on by them from generation to generation, so meticulous memorization was necessary. When we tell a story that represents the collective, it must be accurate.

The story's emotion must feel real, even if it is a battle from a thousand years ago. The key elements have to be both believable and accurate, so others will continue to share the stories and learn the lessons they provide.

Through repetition, a good story gets better, and through retelling it, a storyteller adds in small details, making it relevant. They speak the language of the current generation while staying true to the spirit of the story and its key facts. This helps everyone remember. In turn, they train a new storyteller. And the cycle continues.

The story stays the same, though not everyone is great at remembering and retelling a story.

Have you ever played a game of Chinese Whispers?

A group of people in a circle tell a story, one by one. The first person has the story on a piece of paper and has a minute or two to memorize it, then pass it on by whispering it to the person beside them. They in turn, they do the same, until ten, twenty, or more people have retold the story.

The story at the end is different to from the original. A lot different.

Without a professional storyteller, the story becomes confused. The storyteller role is vital in keeping a historical story true to its original facts and purpose. The pride of a people, battles won and lost, family names, the marriages, the births, and the deaths—all vital to remember and tell correctly.

You can be a storyteller today

The modern storyteller has the benefit of writing out their talk. Of reviewing it. Of storing it and retrieving it later. And of making it available to other people through speech, video, and the written word.

Great, wise storytellers are still consulted by leaders, kings, and captains of business to advise in the present, based on the results of the past.

How many business strategy trainers have we heard refer to The Art of War? And for time management, Steven Covey's "7 Habits" books.

The stories in those books are told and retold, again and again.

The stories we tell will be remembered most when we give a speech, a sales presentation, or a training.

Life is our stories

Our presentation is just a story other people will talk about tomorrow. And since the best part of our presentation will be the stories, these will be the parts they'll repeat to others.

What about the facts? They'll retell the facts via stories.

What about our amazing offer and special pricing? They'll retell the benefits via a testimonial or personal story they heard.

Stories are important, so they should be where we focus most of our speaking time, and if we're are going to tell a lot of stories, making them interesting is integral. We do this through strategic preparation.

For example:

"What did you do on the weekend?"

"Went for a bit of a walk."

"Oh, okay, great."

Vs.

"What did you do on the weekend?"

"I went hiking in the Appalachian mountains, following a three thousand year old trail and saw fossils, ancient native art, and the bluest blue sky of my life."

"Wow, that sounds incredible! How did you find out about this place?"

Which story encourages you to want to hear more? The full, interesting story.

Or how about this:

"Have you traveled much?"

"No."

Silence.

Vs.

"Have you traveled much?"

"Well, for me, I don't think of it as 'much' because I've hardly scratched the surface of the number of places I want to go. But my favorite destination this year was Almaty in Kazakhstan. Did you know more than three hundred thousand Koreans were migrated there after the Korean war, so two generations later, the former Russian culture is heavily influenced by Korea?"

"No. That sounds amazing! Wow, tell me more."

A short story, with some facts and interesting information. Delivered the right way, this could be the beginning of a series of stories.

Good story openings have the audience wanting to hear more.

Let us look at a typical presentation

We can take a logical approach to analyzing the talk:

- It has an introduction
- It has a middle
- It has a conclusion

But this is simplistic and forgets the reason people are paying attention: for the entertainment value.

The three parts would be better prepared as:

- The opening story
- The stories in the middle
- The closing story

Because:

Facts and data are boring; real-life stories give the facts meaning.

The long list of a product's features of a product are boring; seeing people using the product and talking about it is more believable and interesting.

Giving a talk is boring and or intimidating; sharing stories is easy.

Nothing provides more entertainment value than stories.

Want some examples?

"This phone has sixty-four gigabytes of memory and lithium batteries. You can store a lot of data. You will also be able to download a lot of apps. It will have charge when you need it."

Vs.

"I went to the festival, got three hours of video footage, took five hundred selfies—and my phone still isn't flat two days later!"

"This drink has seventeen vitamins, minerals, guarana, and amino acids for health and well-being."

Vs.

"Red Bull gives you wings."

Every presentation becomes a story that can be retold—testimonials, references, customer reviews.

Think about the concept of a presentation, a talk, a training, then think about how hard it is, how much needs to be taught. What key points have to be expressed? What emotions, body language, and volume should we consider?

All of those key points are important, but they're easy to adapt when we tell stories.

Professional Storytelling

If we think about public speaking like this, the fear should go away, because we tell stories every day. Again and again, we tell them to our friends, families, colleagues. We tell them to strangers on the plane. We tell them to our doctors, our dentists, our hairdressers.

What's is one of the simplest ways to tell a story? After something "happens." An accident, an injury, an illness, or something out of the ordinary. The unusual, the entertaining, the challenging, the surprising.

And when do we tell these stories? When someone asks: "What happened to you?"

If I was to ask you "What happened?" just before you picked up this book today, you could tell a story.

If I asked you "What happened" at breakfast this morning, you would have a story.

Everyday life can seem boring until we apply meaning to it.

1Here's how we make stories interesting

"I grew up in a happy family. My parents were loving and caring, and we had a wonderful childhood. I have nothing to complain about."

"I grew up in a broken family. My parents split when I was eleven years old, but we had a wonderful childhood. I have nothing to complain about."

Both these of stories are simplistic. Neither digs into feelings, emotions, specific events, or how they created change, surprise, or anything unexpected.

When the storyteller is simplistic, or unwilling to risk going beneath the surface, all we have is a shallow story.

What everyone wants is a story worth retelling. We want to be amazed, interested, fascinated, or shocked.

Amazing stories take us to places that are out of the ordinary and show us experiences in life we can hardly believe possible. They expand our reality; they challenge us and our way of life.

In addition, interesting stories add knowledge, facts, trivia, and information. In other words, they give us some new input, and we learn things we didn't know before to give us something new to talk about tomorrow. This will, in turn, make us sound more interesting.

Fascinating stories are the ones we stop everything to listen to. When we're fascinated, we lose all other distractions and we're 100% focused. A fascinating story draws us in with its many elements of intrigue, curiosity, and wonder.

Shocking stories make us stop what we are doing and may make us question our attitudes, or conflict with our values and morals. They often contain heartbreak, tragedy, or disaster. They can also involve cruelty, pain, and suffering. Every shocking story needs to have a point, otherwise it is simply "shock value," and all that does is grab the listener's attention. But where to next?

Let us apply these concepts to our family story

Want to make it amazing?

"I grew up in a happy family. My parents' love was expressed every day in so many ways. Through good manners and common courtesies, I learned to respect them, and from an early age, I learned the value of money by being responsible for my purchases. I learned about love from the example they set by serving one another and demonstrating their love in public by holding hands and buying each other small gifts. The videos of our family have become priceless memories since their tragic death when we were teenagers."

Shocking?

"I grew up in a happy family. At least on the surface. Below our shiny, polished veneer lay a culture of distrust, violence, and hatred. But society said parents should stay together, so my mother suffered. My father beat her, and us, every day. We lived in fear, but to the outside world, we looked perfect. Inside, it was a prison."

Fascinating?

"I grew up in a happy family. Even though my parents broke up when I was eleven years old, they both continued to care for us. We had communication with them every day of our teenage years, and now they appear to be better friends than they were all those years ago. I am glad they made the commitment to work on loving us, despite the love they no longer had for each other."

Let's look at the other six storytelling styles we can prepare for our talks to have the audience paying attention and remembering our message.

Secret #2

Funny Stories

Life is funny

We do not plan it that way, but it often is. When we least expect it, life "happens," and a lot of the time, it is funny.

The best stories come straight from life, and the unexpected, unusual, or funny. Funny stories that involve us give our talks authenticity and also connect to many people who have had similar experiences.

How can we can create funny stories?

But first, let me tell you a story

At my public speaking workshops, I like for people to share about their personal strengths. This helps them really see people, to see what the audience connects with and wants more of. We work together to build their self-esteem and create a more powerful image.

At one workshop in Toronto, a woman arrived late to the session. We'd already done the first exercise, where everyone did a short speech. I invited her to share hers with everyone, right then and there. As soon as I got her name, I invited her to introduce herself.

"Hi, my name's Dolores," she said, and everyone in the room responded, "Hi, Dolores!"

"I show people how to make money." Her voice boomed and bellowed, ending with a rumbling laugh just beneath the surface. "And that's real funny, because I ain't got none!"

Then she roared with laughter, and so did the entire room. Everyone in the audience had been learning about how to make a strong first impression. And in three short sentences, Dolores had taught us something: the words we say about ourselves tells the audience how we feel about ourselves.

Would we take financial advice from Dolores? No.

Would we run in the other direction? Yes.

With her initial talk, she was doing what came naturally to her; we weren't setting her up to fail. Everyone had participated in the activity and, along with Dolores, many could see the need to improve. Throughout the workshop, we found ways to make her introduction better. She knew from that day forward, a well-prepared opening would make a big difference in her results.

The story was funny then. When I tell it in front of a live audience, they laugh and get the point. It is more effective than telling the audience like a schoolteacher, and less confrontational. The story gives the lesson.

Another story?

I was giving a workshop in a small country town. About forty people were scattered amongst the chairs and the front row was full. I recognized a few of the people from previous events, and I smiled as I made eye contact with each of those people in the front row.

When the I began the talk, I scanned the group and I made eye contact with this one blonde woman who I knew was a fitness fanatic. She had striking features, and I lingered, smiling. We were friends, so it wasn't uncomfortable.

But then, the strangest thing happened: her eyes widened, and her eyebrows arched. I thought to myself … Interesting!

I continued walking around the room, talking to everyone, making eye contact here and there. When I walked past her again, the same thing occurred: her eyes widened, pupils dilated. Seemed like she was looking at me like I were the best thing she'd ever seen, and she wanted me to know it. This was now a bit disconcerting, so I kept moving.

Finally, on the third pass, I had to stop.

"Do you know what you're doing with your eyes?" I asked.

"What thing?" she said.

"When I look you in the eyes, yours get wider and your eyebrows raise as if you've seen something you really, really, like the look of."

The audience laughed.

"It is the sexiest thing I've ever seen, but is a little distracting."

"I still don't know what you mean," she said.

Her friend turned to her. "You know, that thing with your eyes," she said.

Still unconvinced, the blonde sat and thought about it for about ten seconds, until realization dawned. Her eyes narrowed, and she tilted her head to one side.

"Now I know why my boss has been calling five pm meetings every day. He sits on his desk, and I'm in a chair. The meetings go on, and on, and on. There's nowhere else to look, so I look him in the eye a lot. So he thinks? ... Oh, that's going to change!"

At this, the audience laughed. Then we talked for a while about how the speaker can lead the audience with good body language and eye contact, but sometimes, how the audience can do the leading.

The unexpected ending

Sometimes people expect speakers to be a certain way. They think we will be serious or teach valuable lessons, even over a cup of coffee. Stories can have emotional triggers and stimulate a more powerful memory of a meeting, and this is good when people later on think of the story and the lesson.

If we can tell a funny story, it will be one of the highlights of our talk. When we have multiple funny stories, we aim to create a positive memory of the whole talk.

In my training sessions, I tell a story about people in the audience talking with their hands. I wave my arms around and to simulate the typical expressive person and suggest maybe they put their hands into their pockets. If they have keys or coins in there, it will be a distraction for the audience.

I have coins in my pocket to demonstrate—jingle, jingle, jingle.

But then the twist...

Even without keys or coins in their pockets, if people are nervous, this could be a distraction. Because if we talk with our hands out of our pockets, then we will talk with our hands when they're in our pockets. And if there's no noise, it looks like there is something going on in our pants. This is distracting behavior! Especially when we're making eye contact with the people in our front row!

The audience laughs, embarrassed, because their eyes have been drawn down to "waist" level, and they realize they have become a part of the joke. They get the lesson, because it is a story with an accompanying emotion, visual, and sound.

Finally, something funny we can all prepare

Humor in stories can be by design, but most of the time, the real-life story is funnier, we just need to get the timing right when we tell it. Timing is everything.

We don't need to invent or exaggerate a story. In the right context, some stories are even funnier than we first discovered. Testing it on an audience or two helps us to discover what is funny versus what we think is funny.

Most funny stories happen when people speak without thinking or preparing. They put their foot in their mouth, saying something embarrassing or funny.

In other cases, people say funny things because they slip up, sometimes despite having planned out their phrases, sentences, or jokes. Sometimes it is a question, other times a comment.

The nature of humans is emotion first, logic second (or not at all). While they are being entertained, their logic switches are "off," and their emotional triggers are "on," so what they do and say is innate and reactionary. Reactions are emotional and spontaneous.

We can count on many situations like this being funny, and they are the ones I see in my workshops and as a speaker.

What about other life situations in life that are funny?

- Dating failures
- Eating at the restaurant
- Someone snoring during the opera
- Children in the cinema
- Christmas or Thanksgiving with the family
- Stuff our parents say
- Crazy things our kids say
- What we see people doing in their cars in traffic
- What happened the last time you heard a fire alarm
- Children playing in the park
- Dads playing with kids for the first time
- Dads changing diapers for the first time

Think about the funniest videos on the internet. YouTube would not be the same without cats, puppies, elephants, sloths, and monkeys. But the funniest videos involve children, teenagers, and adults.

- People falling over
- People trying stunts
- People being adventurous
- People getting hurt
- People walking into windows
- People trying to be superheroes

- People who are a little intoxicated
- Kids after they have been to the dentist
- Kids mimicking their parents
- Kids acting out their feelings
- Kids having temper tantrums

Most of these are funny, because we have something in our life we can relate to them. And sometimes the sheer ridiculous nature of what people can get up to do is just … plain funny.

Tell the story, get the laughs. We can lighten up in our presentation with humor. We can link to our product, service, or topic when we tell funny stories, and the memory of the humor will be linked to our product in a positive way.

Incredible Stories - I don't believe it!

"You'll never believe it!"
"I can't believe this is true!"
"I couldn't make this up!"

Coincidences and amazing stories

These are the stories that make our jaws drop, our eyes bulge, and our heads shake. They are so incredible, unbelievable, impossible, and improbable, they have to be true.

Many sayings explain the unusual and amazing:

- "Fiction imitates reality."
- "You can't make this stuff up."
- "Only in America."
- "Well, they are from the country."
- "You know they are only young."
- "How is it so?"

- "Based on a true story."

The human imagination is good, but real life provides us with surprises. Movies are inspired by real stories, dreams, goals, or the imagination.

What fascinates us?

- What people do to each other
- What people do in of anger
- What people do in the heat of passion
- What people do for love
- What happens to people by accident
- What happens to us when we're busy making other plans

Coincidences give us chills down our spine; we are always amazed by the way life creates these strange situations.

Sometimes we may ask ourselves: Is such an amazing story even real? It does not matter. Point is, the audience loves an incredible story. We can always link the story to our point or to our message—fascinating stories have great value to a storyteller.

Urban myths are just as powerful stories as true events. Which they often are. Check out some of these true events and feel free to use them.

You will never believe it

A Saudi woman enlisted the help of her brother to drive her husband's vehicle through red lights; she is planning revenge on the night of his second wedding.

A YouTube video went viral: one of the pickup truck going back and forth through a red light at a Saudi intersection. Social media in the country later reported the truck was being driven by the owner's brother-in-law.

The reports said the owner's wife was angry at her husband for taking a second wife, so she had her brother help her take the truck on the man's wedding night and the pair drove the vehicle through numerous red lights outfitted with traffic cameras, to rack up a total of $80,000 in fines.

What are some other examples of stories that we cannot believe?

Coincidence or chance?

The internet is a great place to find stories, and movies are even made along the same lines.

True love

Serendipity is a movie from 2001, featuring John Cusack and Kate Beckinsale. In it, after her first date goes well, Sarah (Kate) writes her name and phone number inside a book, then donates the book to a second-hand bookstore.

Jon (John) visits every bookstore in the country, hoping to see the name and number he has been longing for.

Many years later, both are engaged to be married. Still, neither can shake the need to give fate one last chance to reunite them, so Jon enlists the help of his best man to track down the girl he can't forget, starting at the store where they met, and Sara flies from California to New York, hoping destiny will bring back her soul mate.

I won't tell you what happens, but you can guess.

An American Woman in Paris

An American writer, Anne Parrish, and her husband were on holiday in Paris in 1920. They were browsing bookshops, and Anne picked up a book that was a particular favorite of hers: "Jack Frost and Other Stories." Anne told her husband that, as a child, her parents had given her a copy, so she had wonderful memories of the book.

Anne's husband took the book, opened it, and there on the inside cover, was a handwritten inscription that read: "Anne Parrish, 209 N Weber Street, Colorado Springs." The inscription was in Anne's handwriting. It was Anne's own book from all those years ago!

Source: *While Rome Burns*, by Alexander Woollcott.

The girl

I met a girl on the train, took her number, and called her. We grew close and talked a lot. It wasn't romance, just a friendship.

A friend of mine at the time told me about a girl he'd had fallen in love with, said I had no idea how much she meant to him. One day, he gave me his phone and I saw a contact number saved by the title "VIP." I was curious, and guess whose number it was? The same number I'd gotten from the girl I'd met on the train! It was an amazing coincidence. Lucky she and I had no intention of dating.

The case of the wrong address

I work at a place where frequent UPS deliveries are made. One day, a driver was having trouble delivering a small package. The address was wrong (wrong zip code

AND a typo in the street name), and it was at the end of a long day.

The driver knew I was familiar with that area and hoped I'd maybe heard of this street, so he handed me the package to check. Lo and behold, it was a package for my father-in-law!

He doesn't even live in the zip code I work in, so it took several coincidences to get that the package on his truck. Then, on the off-chance, he asked if I knew the street. I wasn't even supposed to be at the shop that day, as I was scheduled to be off early.

The UPS driver said that, in twenty-five years of driving, something nothing so bizarre has never happened.

The King's Double

The eighteenth century Italian king, Umberto, went into a restaurant in Monza with General Emilio Ponzia Vaglia, where the owner of the restaurant took King Umberto's order. The king noticed that he and the restaurant owner looked almost identical; they could have almost been brothers.

As they discussed their similarities, they discovered that they'd both been born on March 14, 1844. They'd both been born in the same town, and they had both married women called named Margherita. Plus, the owner had opened his restaurant on the same day Umberto had been crowned king.

A few years later, on the evening of July 29, 1900, King Umberto was told that the restaurant owner had died. As Umberto said how sorry he was to hear this sad news, he was shot four times by assassin Gaetano Bresci.

Just a bit of fun gone wrong

Seems that a while ago, some Boeing employees on the field decided to steal a life raft from one of the 747s. They were successful in getting it out of the plant and back home.

When they took it for a float on the Stilliguamish River, however, they were quite surprised by a coast guard helicopter. It was homing in on the emergency locator that activates when the raft is inflated.

They are no longer employed at Boeing.

Affairs of the heart

As Dorothy Fletcher of Liverpool knows only too well, few places are worse to have a heart attack than on a transatlantic flight. (Unless fifteen of your fellow passengers are cardiologists on their way to a conference.)

In November of 2003, Mrs. Fletcher was flying from Manchester to Florida for her daughter's wedding when disaster struck. The stewards put out an urgent appeal for any doctors on board to make themselves known.

"I couldn't believe what happened," Mrs. Fletcher recalled. "All these people came rushing down the aisle toward me."

The cardiologists kept her stable while the plane was diverted to North Carolina. She even recovered to make it to the wedding.

Catch a falling star

In human history, only one person has been unlucky enough to have been struck by a meteorite. The laws of probability dictate that meteorites will generally fall into uninhabited areas, like deserts or oceans. But this one landed on a woman snoozing on her sofa.

In November 1954, Ann Hodges of Sylacauga, Alabama was asleep in her lounge when suddenly a chunk of space rock crashed through her ceiling and hit her. It caused an enormous bruise on her thigh, but she was otherwise unharmed.

"You have a better chance of getting hit by a tornado, and a bolt of lightning, and a hurricane all at the same time," astronomer Michael Reynolds told National Geographic.

Time for a lottery ticket?

We will meet again

A woman in Gwent spent years trying to track down her long-lost brother, but was amazed when she discovered he lived right across the road from her house!

Rose Davies had been raised by foster parents and had only later been told she had three brothers. Sid and John had been easy to find, but there was no trace of Chris.

Little did she know that she had already befriended him and his family.

"I had only known them for three months," she commented, "but I thought they were nice."

Twins

Twins Jim Lewis and Jim Springer, were separated at birth and adopted by different families. Unbeknownst to each other, both families had named the boys James. Each James had grown up not knowing of the other, yet both had sought law enforcement training. Each had the ability in mechanical drawing and carpentry, and each had married a woman named Linda. Each had sons, one of whom was named James Alan and the other was named James Allan. Each had also divorced his first wife and remarried another woman—named Betty. And each owned a dog named Toy.

Amazing stories are entertaining, and the person telling the story, and the person listening, both benefit.

We can insert amazing stories into our own presentations

When we hear a song played from our past, it reminds us of boyfriends, girlfriends, school, jobs, and our youth; school dances, first kisses, exams, sports, and more. Every memory can stimulate a new story.

If we are in sales, amazing stories can link to the amazing benefits of our product, or we might have an amazing story of our own.

Coincidences can be linked to the element of chance and luck, and we can compare them to the strategies of the deliberate, methodical, and successful entrepreneurs of the world.

Remember, amazing stories are easier to remember than simple facts. Make your stories funny, incredible, and unbelievable so everyone will share them with their friends.

Secret #3

The Past and the Present

When I was young, I wanted to be a public speaker

I studied the art of speaking and modeled myself after some of my idols, Og Mandino, Jim Rohn, and Denis Waitley.

I would read books, listen to audio cassettes, and sit in the audience to learn from every presenter.

I had made the decision to be a speaker, but it took me another seven years to get up on the stage and teach and train audiences around Australia.

Two years later, I began my international speaking career. Every year, my speaking audience became more diverse. From Australia and New Zealand to Southeast Asia, the USA and Canada, Europe and Central Asia. Now, I am proud to say I have achieved my goal as international speaker, trainer, and author, working in over 20 countries, and visiting more than 40 so far.

When I was young, I learned to play the piano

From the age of fourteen, every Monday night I took lessons from David, my music teacher. I got better very quickly. I started at AMEB (Australian Musical

Examinations Board) in fourth grade, and finished three years later at the equivalent of eighth grade.

Each week, David would tell me how well I was progressing, which was surprising, as I hardly practiced at all. I hated scales. My method of single-handed learning was inefficient and didn't accelerate my learning at the speed of other students. I was just lucky, or had enough raw talent, to bluff my way through, week by week.

After a year of lessons, I thought I could pull off being a classical pianist, performing in front of audiences around the world. That was, until I found out how much they practiced each day (six to eight hours). And I was struggling to commit to 30 minutes!

So instead, I learned to play other tunes. I played at church. I played at friends' houses and at parties. I even played at home along with the radio and TV.

Then came my big break. On Boxing Day, while still just seventeen years old, I played for three hours in a piano bar called Pippins, at the Terminus Hotel in Shepparton. I stayed for two hours after, until the bar closed at midnight.

I was home—a piano, a bar, people relaxing, and me entertaining them.

I was invited back for New Year's Eve, when I played for five hours and had songs requested by beautiful women. People tipped me for playing songs they wanted. It was awesome.

The next four years I put myself through university just playing piano. I played for five hours every Saturday, and even started teaching high school students on my days off.

The piano overpaid me for the few years of practice. I am glad I had enough discipline to sit and pass all four exams.

"When I was young."

It is a simple opening for a story. It refers both to a time we remember, and a time our audience can relate to.

We can all tell these stories, because we know them as our childhood, and our audience will empathize, putting themselves into the story.

> Everyone was young,
> Everyone was a child,
> Everyone was a teenager,
> Everyone had parents.

The most simple story to tell is from our first memories; every defining moment in our lives shines out like a spotlight from our timeline.

Every life-changing decision we made changed our life, creating either pain or pleasure. Every relationship we started or finished is a story, and every dream and goal we've had has created who we are today.

When we share these stories, our audience will go back to the same time in their lives. This is a secret strategy for gaining rapport with our audience.

What are some of the things we did when we were young that could be shared in a story?

Sport

- When I was young, I used to play cricket, but I was never good enough to make it to the A grade. I still loved to play, though.
- When I was young, I never played any sport, and now my body is paying the price. My #1 regret is not being active in my youth.

- When I was young, I wanted to play basketball, but I was too short and slow. Now, I've found a sport that I do not need to be tall for: being a jockey.

- When I was young, I wanted to be a downhill skier, but I lived in the middle of the desert. I moved to Aspen, Colorado at the age of eighteen and never left.

- When I was young, I wanted to play tennis, but we didn't have enough money for lessons. So I hit the ball against the side of our garage until I was old enough to get a job and pay for lessons myself.

- When I was young, I swam every summer day for fun, but never for competitions. A scout found me, coached me, and now I am swimming at my second Olympic Games.

- When I was young, I kicked a football every waking moment, 365 days a year. I joined a team as soon as I could, becoming captain in my second year.

- When I was young, I watched my idols on TV and dreamed of being on stage. Now, I stand on stage in front of thousands of people.

- When I was young, I saw my football idols live. It reinforced my passion to play when I grew up.

- When I was young, I had a famous cricketer sign my hat at a big game, and I never washed it again. I still love cricket and everything that goes with it.

Our childhood is a time of innocence, so the stories we tell from then are innocent, too.

Note that all of the sentences above are just the opening to a story that could be as long or as short as we want.

What other things happened when we were young?

We learned

- When I was young, I learned to play the piano. I didn't like it much, so I quit.

- When I was young, I learned to play the guitar. I loved its sound and practiced every day.

- When I was young, I learned to cut the grass using a lawn mower, which became my first part-time job.

- When I was young, I learned to prune roses so they'd flower better in the spring.

- When I was young, I learned to grow vegetables in our backyard, so we always had giant zucchini and watermelon.

- When I was young, I learned another language, and I've been able to speak fluent Spanish ever since.

What else did we learn? Well, not everything was learned when we were young children. We learn new things as teenagers, too.

Teenage years

- When I was a teenager, I learned that girls don't like it when you throw things at them.

- When I was a teenager, I learned that some bodies changed faster than others. For three years, I was the shortest person in high school.

- When I was a teenager, I wanted to kiss a girl, but not all girls were the same. Some wanted to, and some didn't.

- When I was a teenager, I thought school was everything. I loved learning and wanted to become a teacher.

- When I was a teenager, I couldn't wait to drive a car. I practiced on farms and back roads until I had the skills to take my driving test and drive legally.

- When I was a teenager, I learned to ride a motorcycle. Not well—I rode it into the fence the first time. But then I got back on and learned how to ride safely.

- When I was a teenager, I left home for university in the big city. All my of friends and family were left behind for this new adventure.

- When I was a teenager, I discovered for the first time boys wanted to date me. I had to have the conversation with my friends about what to do, because my mother was distant.

- When I was a teenager, I learned school subjects were not preparing me for real life, so I started to read books by Robert Kiyosaki and Brian Tracy.

- When I was a teenager, I learned how gossip and bullying could destroy someone. I was on the receiving end and I also dished it out.

- When I was a teenager, I rebelled and ran away from home. I ended up, for just one day, in a town just 40 kilometers away before I was found and taken home.

- When I was a teenager, I became an alcoholic. I have now been sober for 20 years.

- When I was a teenager, I left my family home and spent twelve months overseas on student exchange. It was a great experience where I gained friends and learned a new language.

- When I was a teenager, I learned how to build a computer. I saved a lot of money for myself, and plus made money building them for friends and local businesses.

- When I was a teenager, I learned that being a geek could be cool when you fixed girls' phones for them.

We were younger five minutes ago than we are now. We can use this same formula in recent years, even if we are in our forties, fifties, or even older.

- When I was thirty-three years old, I decided I wanted to stay this age forever.
- When I received my thirty-eighth birthday gift from my son, I was happy, because it was a ticket to the Formula 1 Grand Prix in Monaco.
- When I was forty, my family threw a big party. "Life begins now," they said.
- When I was forty-four, I remember thinking: life does not get any better than this.
- When I was forty-seven, I sold my first business for 33 million dollars.
- When I was fifty, I reflected on my achievements and smiled, while lying on the beach in the Bahamas.
- When I turned sixty-five, I knew I couldn't retire yet. There was still too much work to do.
- When I turned sixty-nine, I knew retirement was still a long ways away. I couldn't afford to stop working, since I had no savings.

So we can relive our past and use it as a point of reference from which our stories start. Then, once we've told it, we can make our points or show the story's relevance.

But let's go back to the impact other people have had on us when we were young.

Who taught us?

Most of our early influencers were our parents, before grandparents, aunts, and uncles became more involved. Then our teachers, coaches, tutors, and lecturers all got involved in our lives. Lastly, our boyfriends, girlfriends, spouses, bosses, colleagues, and life itself provided lessons.

Someone new will teach us tomorrow, and then we will have another story.

What did they teach us?

When I was young, my mother taught me to have good manners, to always say "please" and "thank you." This was common sense advice, and it became a habit that has always been good to remember around the world. In fact, those are the two words I learn first in any language of a country I am speaking in.

When I was young, my father taught me to type. I didn't want to; it was difficult on the old-fashioned, clunky typewriters we had in school. Learning to touch-type, though, was the best business skill I could develop, outside of sales and marketing.

Being able to type at 60 words per minute while sitting in a cafe lets me write books as I watch the world go by. It has helped me write more than a dozen books and thousands of pages of websites and training materials.

When I was young, my grandmother taught me to love cooking. Most Sundays we would cook cakes, biscuits, slices, and other delicious snacks. We would eat so much. But the best part was she would let us take home the extras.

I have loved cooking ever since, and for most of my adult life, I've been the first into the kitchen.

When I was young, my grandfather taught me to use my brain. When we visited, he would sit me down in front of complex crossword puzzles, wanting to make me think and solve these cryptic challenges. It built my vocabulary and expanded my world of language.

Ever since then, no challenge in front of me has seemed impossible. When a six-year-old solves a cryptic crossword, they feel invincible. I will never forget thinking it was impossible back then, and now I remember there is always a solution.

When I was young, my first boss taught me to work hard and to take instruction. It was hard at first, after having such a carefree childhood. But that job trained me to work hard from the minute the sun came up, to when it set. For the rest of my life, I will never say a farmer is ever lazy.

When I was young, I got a job working in a factory and learned the value of cleaning. Whenever I see a dirty workplace, I see someone not doing their job. When the cleaner has pride in their work, the rest of the workplace shines and is more valuable to the staff and visitors.

When I was young, I learned the power of working in a team—sports teams, community work teams, academic teams, bands. This helped me to work on projects later in life and delegate wherever necessary. I learned to identify the strengths of each team member and use his skill set in the right position.

All of these stories help people tap into their own childhood. When they do, they remember what they learned about life, living, and loving. We can prompt this by asking them a question after our story: "What did you learn?"

What else did we do when we were young?

We've all lived in different places. It is the question people ask about us when they we meet. "Where are you from?" We can tell stories about where we were born and where we have lived. The location forms part of our history, and it may even define our personality, accent, or view on life.

When I was young, I lived in Canberra, the capital of Australia. Every day I would ride my bike around roads pre-built to anticipate the city doubling in size in the next twenty years. And it did. When I was young, though, I had the freedom to discover entire suburbs even before a single house had been built.

When I was young, my parents broke up and we moved away from Canberra to Shepparton. That town of just 23,000 people was came as a culture shock. I had left a clean, purpose-built city of bureaucrats and public servants and was smack-bang in the middle of a regional community of Italians.

When I was young, we moved six times in eighteen months, becoming local nomads, all while I prepared for my final year exams. I had to focus on the present amidst the chaos of our home life. In my final high school year, I achieved my best academic and sporting results, including becoming school vice-captain and house captain.

When I was young, I moved away from the country to the big city. From my relaxed country lifestyle around 23,000 people, I was in the big city of Melbourne with over three million people. A new type of culture shock, but one I learned to love. I loved the pulsing energy of a city that never slept.

When I was young, I got a passport and took my first overseas trip to Manila in the Philippines. I had no idea what it would be like, but I was excited to travel and that first trip has led to over two million kilometers of visiting people and places around the world.

Want other examples? How about family-related topics? Think about a story we can tell by focusing on these words:

Vacations and holidays

- When I was young, we went to the beach for vacation and…
- When I was young, we went overseas for our vacations, which was good because…
- When I was young, we went to the city and saw…
- When I was young, we visited the country and discovered…
- When I was young, we didn't have much, so our vacation was always…
- When I was young, we were richer than other kids in town, and our school vacation was always…
- When I was young, we couldn't afford to go on a vacation so we had to…
- When I was young, we had foster children in our home, so school vacations meant…
- When I was young, we built a cubby house in the backyard on our vacation…

Got any favorites?

- When I was young, my favorite toy was…
- When I was young, my favorite friend was…
- When I was young, my favorite food was…
- When I was young, my favorite weekend activity was…

- When I was young, my favorite sport was
- When I was young, my favorite TV show was…
- When I was young, my favorite band was…
- When I was young, my favorite movie star was…
- When I was young, my favorite…

Firsts

- When I was young, my first …
- When I was young, my first day at school…
- When I was young, my first kiss…
- When I was young, my first boyfriend…
- When I was young, my first tragedy…
- When I was young, my first acting performance…
- When I was young, my first reality check…
- When I was young, my first success…
- When I was young, my first exam…
- When I was young, my first job…

We can all start our stories with "When I was young" to get the audience to pay attention.

It is important that we to link our opening to the topic or to the point of our presentation. This way, the audience will continue to listen. We don't tell a story to grab their attention, and then change the topic. They will feel manipulated. We need to link it to the point of our talk.

We should have enough stories from these examples to fill days of workshops or speeches. If we take the time to tell a few of them in early in our speech we will gain rapport and have them nodding, smiling, and feeling comfortable.

We need to practice a story and start sharing it. This will keep our audience interested and the stories will sound fresh. Fresh like it is the first time it has been told.

So, no matter how old we are, we can all use: "When I was young."

What about the future?

Not every talk needs to start with the past. We can focus on the future, to paint a picture with our words and have people see what we are talking about.

When we do this, we take people out of their current situation. This can be good if we are showing things can be different or better in the future.

- When I am forty, I want to be retired. To make that happen, I will do this now…
- When I am fifty, I plan to live in the Caribbean. My strategy for being able to live on an island is simply this…
- In two years' time, I will have five books published, and create a residual income. So two years ago, I started writing and my first book already makes money every month. How you can do this too is…
- In five years, I will have created five millionaires through my mentoring and coaching.
- In twenty years, I hope to be the most active grandfather on the planet. My exercise plan…
- In thirty years, I still plan on being in love, because I will do these three things every day.

The future is a wonderful place to tell stories, because they're are all, in some part, imaginary.

Making them more real requires showing a plan, a strategy, and a commitment.

When we're are confident in the future, other people will be, too. We need to have stories about our future, because they'll will become the stories of our past.

Secret #4

Other People's Stories

When we tell a personal story, we captivate the audience. They are getting an insight that can be both intimate and emotional, and it brings them into a private world they feel respectful and privileged to be listening to.

Telling our own stories are the easiest; they are the ones we know the best. Our next best stories are those of the people closest to us: our friends and family

If we do the research, we will realize they can fit our talk perfectly. We can bring a personal experience of a third party to life and relate it to our presentation.

What are some of the general topics we can refer to? Just look at the personal stories of our lives, and those of our family and friends.

Relationships
School
Friends
Family
Travel
Sport
Love
Loss
Work

The best stories relate to a specific moment in time and include other characters and personalities. These make the stories compelling.

Consider the "firsts"

- Our first love
- Our first job
- Our first boyfriend
- Our first girlfriend
- Our first broken heart
- Our first school report
- Our first "A"
- Our first failure
- Our first child
- Our first wedding
- Our first date
- Our first sale
- Our first credit card
- Our first plane ride
- Our first train ride
- Our first overseas trip
- Our first crush
- Our first coffee
- Our first drink
- Our first language lesson
- Our first painting class
- Our first reaction to ballet or opera
- Our first note on the piano

Firsts are nostalgic, and the reaction of others is what makes the story more interesting.

And the best part of that is we can trigger an emotion. When there's an emotional element to a story, the audience engages and pays attention as if it was happening in the present moment.

My first love

My first love in high school was also the girl whose heart I broke. After eighteen months together, I left our country town for the big city, university, and adulthood. The relationship was great, we learned a lot, and we shared many experiences. When the time came and we were going to be living two hundred kilometers apart from each other, breaking up seemed to be the right thing to do. It was the hardest decision I'd ever had to make.

What is the hardest decision you have had to make?

My first child

Benjamin decided to have an adventurous journey into the world. After more than eighteen hours of labor, he was still staying put. The doctors accelerated the birth process as his heart rate was going up to dangerous levels. When he was born, he had the umbilical cord wrapped around his neck not once, but twice. He was grey, and made a reasonable amount of noise as he entered the warm hospital room.

He spent three days inside the humidicrib under constant observation. His mass dropped further, losing 15% of his birth weight of 5lb 6oz before beginning to work out how to feed. Then, after having his first bath, he thought life was for living! He began to grow and develop like normally, putting on weight from that day forward.

Today, he is an independent young man, living in the big city and taking on the world.

Despite his dramatic entrance into the world, Ben has an easy-going attitude toward life today.

We can never let our past determine our future. If we do, it takes away our personal ability to control our destiny through choice.

What happened in your past and is stopping you from living the life you want?

My first credit card

When I was in my first year of university, I was offered and accepted a Visa card with a $1000 limit. At eighteen, I had little money and only a part-time job. It seemed like an easy option to get some cash. In the moment, decisions like this are focused on the present, not the future.

Travel beckoned. My father was living in Brunei, on the island of Borneo in the South China Sea and I visited him over Christmas for a few weeks. On the way home, I had a stopover in Singapore.

Now, this was in the days before credit cards had telephone authorizations, when they used the old "click-clack" imprint machine. Triplicate copies of each sale were issued for the bank, the vendor, and the customer. Generation X and Baby Boomers will remember.

I started the day with a brand-new CD player. It was amazing: a Sony Discman with Xtra-Bass for only $599. (This is about $1400 today)

We weren't yet using the computers at university for our projects, so we had to type them out, so … $300 for an electric typewriter? Good deal.

My favorite music was less than $10 per cassette, so I got about fifteen of them. And a few CDs, too—another $100.

If you're adding this up, you might be realizing by now things are getting out of control. With no rules and in a shopping paradise, I was in heaven. $1000 limit? Ha!

I then found a camera for about $200.

One more stop to go: Plaza Singapura—the Yamaha store.

I saw a DX-7 Keyboard and I knew: this was something I had to have. (No logic stopping me.)

I was working in piano bars and cafes for my part-time job. The keyboard was $1200. I didn't even think twice.

I had no cash left for the subway back up Orchard Road, so I walked the 1.5 kilometers back to the Holiday Inn on Scotts Road carrying everything in 32 degrees Celsius (90F) with 80% humidity. I got to the room, dripping in sweat, just in time to pack my bag and head to the airport on the shuttle bus.

Arriving in Australia about ten hours later, I had a little more than my $400 duty-free allowance. I had to leave the keyboard at the airport for two weeks to make money to then pay the customs duty and retrieve my precious keyboard.

That day in Singapore, I spent over $2500 and it took me six months to pay off the credit card debt. It took so long to pay it back, I had to sell my other electric piano to avoid even greater penalties.

What did I learn?

Eighteen-year-olds have no self-restraint.
Spending without rules creates chaos.
Credit cards cost you long after your purchases if you do not pay them off right away.

Lesson after lesson came out of this one experience. Painful at the time, it has helped me make wiser decisions in financial matters ever since.

These are all true stories. Personal stories are great.

But what about the other people in our life? How can we tell stories about other people and get the same impact?

Every story we have in this format, we can use to engage our audience.

Every persons' stories will be different; they may have a different outcome, a new point to make, something they have learned from a similar experience.

After telling our stories, we can ask our friends and family to share theirs. With their permission we can use their stories in our presentations.

Put on our reporters hat, voice recorder in hand, and ask.

"Please tell me about your first..."

- Your first love
- Your first job
- Your first relationship
- Your first business
- Your first computer
- Your first phone
- Your first break-up
- Your first school report that was not perfect
- Your first "F"
- Your first invention failure
- Your first sleepover
- Your first nightmare
- Your first wedding night

- Your first date as an adult
- Your first car
- Your first house
- Your first credit card
- Your first plane ride
- Your first visit to the city
- Your first overseas trip
- Your first big rejection
- Your first coffee
- Your first cigarette
- Your first beer
- Your first ballet lesson
- Your first visit to the ballet
- Your first book
- Your first reaction to the ocean
- Your first reaction to snow
- Your first experience of another language
- Your first New Year's Eve party
- Your first Christmas

What about the other information we can get from people? Well, we just need to ask.

Tell me about who, when, why, which, what:

- When you were young
- When you were a teenager
- When you started college
- When you lost a sibling
- What you learned from your father

- What the last thing you remember your grandfather saying was
- Why you admired your mother
- Who your favorite relative was
- Who inspired you at school
- Which direction you took after school
- What job offers you received
- How you dealt with rejection
- When you realized you had grown up
- Where you travelled first

If we asked ten people these questions, we would have plenty of stories to use. We could discuss the philosophy of a particular generation, or we could summarize the thoughts of employees in a business. We could even get inside the minds of homeless people living on the streets.

Asking questions is fascinating, if we gather the information and then report on it in a useful way.

Who can we tell unique and interesting stories about?

Our father
Our mother

My father

I have a lot of stories about my father, from my earliest days. He was always playing sports, building things with electronics, and learning about computers.

What stories could I tell?

Learning to play Squash in my pajamas after his game ended at 9 pm.

Learning to type on a typewriter with ribbon and ink and colored paper.

Riding bikes around Canberra; learning to ride fast and to stop fast.

Stories from when I was a teenager are different. We lived with our mother about a six-hour drive from his home and I only saw him three or four times per year. Each time was the perfect environment for having adventures and creating stories I would treasure and replay in the months in-between visits.

Discovering the world of the VCR and movies on VHS cassettes
Playing games on the Commodore 64 computer
Sailing on the lake in Canberra
Learning to windsurf

My mother

My mother and I were close, and because I was the oldest child, I spent the most time with her. When my brother and sister came along, however, I was the natural person to take care of them. Proud and confident, I would answer the phone, help make meals, and be a good eldest son.

My mother taught me to be responsible with money. From the age of fourteen, I managed my own allowance, and bought my own clothes and snacks.

My mother encouraged me to get a part-time job. This made sense, because the only money I would have, had to come from what I earned.

My mother encouraged me to apply for a scholarship to university. I got it.

My mother worked hard for many years as a single parent. She supported and nurtured me, my sister, and baby brother.

My mother was always available to listen as I navigated through my teenage years.

Each of these openings can lead to a ten-minute story and people will relate to them, because everyone had a mother.

What if we run out of stories of our own?

Should we just make up stories? This is harder than it seems. True stories are easy to remember. They are more interesting, because of the reality factor. Remember, the most amazing and incredible stories are from real life.

Maybe we need to find people in our life and ask to hear their stories. Then retell them with their permission.

The best-selling books of all time tell the same stories. Audiences likes to hear the "old favorites" sometimes.

- Thomas Edison and the light bulb
- Leonardo DaVinci and his inventions
- Einstein's theory of relativity
- Alexander Bell and the telephone
- Madame Curie and radiation therapy
- Mother Teresa caring for people in the slums of Calcutta
- Princess Diana supporting the removal of land mines

We can hear famous stories every day, stories anyone can look up on the internet and copy from. This is lazy speaking and if we want to stand out, we will need to work harder than the average speaker.

Stories about other famous people are okay for us to hear, but there's is a better and a more effective way to use them.

There are many unique people with unique stories, and we can often link their stories to the point we want to make in our talk.

Many of life's lessons come from our observations of other people.

Who else can we tell stories about?

- Our siblings and how we felt about them
- Our school teachers, including most and least favorite
- Our football coach or sporting teammates
- Our ballet teacher and their strict discipline
- Our piano teacher and their love of music
- Our partners in the school prom or debutante ball
- Our first boss and what we learned from them
- Our co-workers in our first or any other job
- The school bully and how we related to them
- The wimpy kid at work everyone picked on
- Our girlfriend's father and how that first meeting went
- Our boyfriend's mother and how hard it was to get away from her
- The scary neighbor everyone was afraid of
- The priest or pastor at our local church or at school
- The college professor who inspired us or put us to sleep
- The girlfriend's ex we found out about too late
- The boyfriend's ex and why he likes us so much
- The school principal and the meetings we had in his/her office

- The police officer and his/her role in shaping our teen years
- The shop assistant we saw every day before catching the bus
- The performer at the concert who looked into our eyes
- The janitor at school and how we teased him
- The telemarketer on the phone last night
- The pop-up chat person on the website we cannot escape
- The check-in person at the airport with the amazing attitude
- The bus driver who let us ride for free when we had no change
- The pilot who made us feel calm when there was turbulence
- The flight attendant who helped make us comfortable
- Our best friend and their trust in us throughout our life
- Our archenemy and how that turned around ten years later
- Our grandparents and their home and all its smells

Everything that happens to us is a story that is a part of our lives, and we can apply meaning to every story when we remember and retell them well.

Everyone we meet has his or her own story. When that story moves us or affects us, we now have a new part to share in our presentation. Telling that new story may just help everyone in our audience get the point and help the talk move forward.

Who else can we talk to and get new stories when we run out of friends and close family?

- Relatives
- Janitors
- Cooks
- Coaches
- Fitness trainers
- Doctors
- Nutritionists
- Bosses
- Retirees
- Children
- Teenagers
- People with a disability
- Ferry drivers
- Pilots
- Coffee shop owners
- Waiters
- Nurses
- UBER drivers
- Hotel Concierges
- Olympic athletes
- Tour de France riders
- Newspaper delivery boys

The source of new stories is all around us. Unlimited possibilities. There are no excuses when we have the way to start stories.

Now it is time to go and talk to someone and ask them to share their stories with us.

Secret #5

Emotional Stories

Every good story is emotional

We want to tell a story that people can remember and share. Emotion is a powerful tool we can use to create memorable stories.

We want to stimulate an emotional reaction from our audience, which means including information and experiences that have been emotional for us.

Half the battle is being willing to share. Our experiences with the emotions and feelings associated with those stories are powerful. When we show the emotion, the audience may reflect it back to us, or they can at least empathize and feel how we felt.

We must remember, when we have an emotional story, it needs to have a point, something the audience can connect to. Emotion is not enough to make a good story; even when the emotion is positive, we need to link it.

Emotions can create a roller coaster ride for the audience: we get them engaged, take them through it, and out the other side.

This is why the story needs to be well-planned and then well-delivered to achieve the emotional impact and to achieve the outcome we are looking for.

What are some of the emotions or their associative actions we can include in our stories?

- Joy
- Passion
- Happiness
- Success
- Achievement
- Recognition
- Courage
- Irony
- Love
- Unrequited love
- Broken heart
- Lost love
- Cold as ice
- Compassion
- Vulnerability
- Sadness
- AngerFear

Each of these can provide a reaction in our audience. But to get the audience to feel the same emotion at the same time, we have to string them together. How do we do this?

In a movie

Movies "move" us. When we write and share emotional stories as movies, they have power.

What is in a great movie?

Drama. Action. Emotion.

If we can make our stories read like a movie script, the audience will find them irresistible.

The best themes for us to create our stories from? Action and drama—with an element of fantasy. Comedies do not win many academy awards, but action and drama movies do and they attract the big names actors, and create the big paydays.

Success at the box office?

Star Wars Episode VII - action and drama, over $2 billion
Lord of the Rings Trilogy - action and drama, over $2.5 billion
The Avengers I & II - action and drama, over $3 billion
Harry Potter movies 7 & 8 - action and drama, over $2.5 billion

How about at the awards shows:?

The Pianist - drama in wartime, 3 Oscars
The English Patient - drama in wartime, 9 Oscars
The Last Emperor - drama set in the 1920s - 9 Oscars

Stories that become movies we love sell a lot of tickets and they win awards because they create an emotional response in us. These reactions help us to connect to our feelings and make life interesting.

Movies have stars, they have villains and they have tension and resolution—there is a formula, a sequence, a style. Movies capture the audience and take them on an emotional journey.

When we learn to tell stories in the style of a movie, the audience will be listening with their eyes, ears, hearts, and minds.

Every movie moves us. We just need to choose which type of movie we are going to show, and which emotions we want to trigger.

A quick note on context

The movies we create need to fit our talk and be relevant in a way that will make the audience feel comfortable.

We have to find a story that will paint the pictures of the message we want to get across, so we may need to develop characters, show their flaws and imperfections. Typical themes include finding love, losing something of value, or even death and rebirth.

Danger

Danger, risk, adventure, and drama all tap into the vicarious part of a listener. Watching the movie in their mind, they wish they were there to see it, and they count on our storytelling ability to paint the picture and make it real.

We are not just telling a story. We are making a movie.

The thrill of this type of story is the nature of it being something they see themselves in. While watching a movie is safer than being in it, the danger and excitement have their hearts beating faster and their eyes wide open. They are absorbed. Nothing distracts them.

Dangerous stories may involve accident, injury, or death. They involve fear, courage, and action. We are all amazed by dangerous stories because they take us out of our everyday life and we are transported into something and somewhere fantastic.

What are some danger-filled stories that grab our attention?

- Stories about climbing Mt. Everest
- Stories about dramatic fights and arguments
- Stories about natural disasters
- Story about car chases and criminals
- Story about international ripoffs and scams
- Stories about the drug trade
- Stories about the US/Mexico border crossings
- Stories about people smuggling
- Stories about hunting for Osama bin Laden
- Stories about plane crashes
- Stories of hotel fires
- Stories about ferries sinking
- Stories about runaway trains
- Stories about the threat of nuclear war

Dangerous stories link to themes like:

- Risk
- Reward
- Heroism
- Fear
- Courage
- Bravery
- Being under pressure

- Setting an example
- Leadership
- Sacrifice
- Creativity

Being quite open and direct with the link, we can link these stories. People will be in the story, so we need to isolate our characters and explain what we have learned from their behavior.

Did someone rush into a burning building to rescue a child? That is a story of courage, selflessness, and sacrifice. Maybe even a story of love if the person is rescuing a family member.

How about when a natural disaster, like a volcano or a flood destroys a city? It can be a message about losing the past, and having to create a new future; about loss, grief, anger, and the lessons from an event that is beyond our control. Letting go and starting over.

How about another example:

Every day we hear stories in the news about refugees escaping a regime or poverty to find a new home in a new country. These are the stories of desperation, courage, sacrifice, culture, national pride, separation, love, and desire.

When we tell true stories with these emotions, we can capture the audience's attention.

The formula

We need to make these stories into a movie following a proven system or strategy.

An emotional connection with the material needs to be made, or the listener will stop listening. They will stop "watching." And then the movie is finished. Or in our case, the talk is over.

In the movies, one series of stories unfolds as a part of the bigger picture, plot, or screenplay. Along the way, different subplots become parallel, interweaving storylines. But the movie is designed to be a story we tell other people, so we can discuss it, argue with it, fall in love with it, be inspired. Or entertained.

We do not have to reinvent the wheel. All of the road maps make it easy for us to write our own stories and deliver them live to our audiences.

The following statement describes the traits of a great movie director. It works here, too, describing a great storyteller:

1. Have complete confidence in yourself and faith in your talent and ability.
2. Have the courage and tenacity to stick it out "no matter what."
3. Have a relentless focus on what is possible rather than what is not possible.
4. Never stop searching for your unique voice, style, and expression.
5. Stay true to yourself: it will guide you to the right people and the right choices.

(Peter D. Marshall, from his 7-step, film-directing formula)

One formula common in stories that capture the audience's imagination is "The Hero's Journey." Most people recognizes this in *"Star Wars," "The Hunger Games," "The Princess Bride"* and in other action/adventure/drama movies.

"The Hero's Journey" refers to a universal pattern found in stories around the world

"A hero ventures forth from the world of everyday life into supernatural wonder. Amazing and unreal forces are met. There are battles and challenges, both in the heart and in the mind. People may die. Others may fall in love. But in the end, victory is won. The hero comes back from this adventure with wisdom and understanding. They have a newfound maturity and are a changed person..."

The same formula divides a story into a three-act structure: the setup, the confrontation, the resolution.

ACT ONE (set up)
EXAMPLE: "Person finds business opportunity."
1. What is the story plot and the story theme?
2. What is the "dramatic question" to answer?
3. Who is the main character and what are their needs and goals?

ACT TWO (confrontation)
EXAMPLE: "They experience rejection and misunderstanding, as they learn the skills to master this new type of business."
1. What is the dramatic "rising" action?
2. What are the obstacles in the main character's way?
3. How does the main character overcome each obstacle?

ACT THREE (resolution)
EXAMPLE: "Financial and emotional success is achieved. All of their dreams come true, new strong friendships created."
1. How does the story end?
2. What happens to the main character?
3. Is the dramatic question answered?

Can we do the same in our stories? Can we make a movie with this three-point storytelling formula?

How about a few examples:.

ACT ONE:
Boy meets girl

ACT TWO:
Boy tries to impress girl, but gets rejected and has to fight past other options she has. Re-prioritizes around his work schedule to find a way to attract her. Maybe he discovers his inner charm and character.

ACT THREE:
Boy and girl (or boy and boy, or girl and girl) live happily ever after.

Or:

ACT ONE:
Child performs in local play and is admired for acting skill. Desires to go to Hollywood.

ACT TWO:
Child attends many auditions. Gets rejected. Keeps learning. Waits for lucky break. Almost dies trying. Down to last four bucks before performing dramatic poses on Venice Beach and being spotted by a Hollywood producer.

ACT THREE:
Teenager earns millions of dollars after appearing in vampire/ love story/ melodrama on TV for seven seasons.

When we tell a story, we cannot break this proven formula, or the audience will not respond. Everyone has been conditioned to expect the introduction, the challenge or dispute, and the resolution.

In relationship stories—the meeting. The initial positive reaction, then rejection, and then the work to be respected. In the end, total acceptance and "happily ever after."

Here is some more information on movie-making and storytelling

A Hollywood formula story follows the interactions of three characters and still uses the three-act structure.

The Protagonist—this is the person the story is about. He or she is a person who wants a goal. The goal must be something concrete, definable, and achievable. Rather than "I want to be happy" or "I want to be rich," it is "I want him to fall in love with me so that I will be happy," or "I want to win the game show I am going to be on, so that I will be rich." Or even "I want to rob the casino of the guy who's dating my ex-girlfriend, so I can be happy and rich."

The Antagonist—the person who places obstacles to the goal in the protagonist's path. This does not necessarily mean "the bad guy." The antagonist's goals are in some way opposed to the protagonist's own and he or she is the one who is blocking the protagonist's journey.

The Relationship Character—the person who accompanies the protagonist on his or her journey. This is someone who has "been there, done that" before. He or she has the wisdom to communicate to the protagonist, but the protagonist does not pay attention. The theme or lesson of the story is expressed either by or to this character. Ironically, in order to succeed, it is what the protagonist needs to learn. In many cases, this is a conversation. Watching the movie, people are yelling at the protagonist to understand. At the end of the story, this conversation or expression of the theme will be revisited, and the protagonist and this character will reconcile with each other.

The story ends when the protagonist either achieves or relinquishes his or her goal, either defeats or is defeated by the antagonist, and finally reconciles with the relationship character. The closer together these things happen, the more emotional impact the story will have, often in the last five minutes of the movie.

How about the three acts?

If we use them in our story, it will tick all of the storytelling formula boxes.

First Act: beginning of the story. It introduces the characters and their goals. After 10%-15%, the protagonist faces a fateful decision, a choice. How they answer determines whether or not there is a story.

Second Act: a quarter of the story has already been told. Problems start to pile on. Up until the halfway point, the story has been raising questions. From here on, it begins to answer them.

Third Act: three-quarters or more of the story has already been told. The beginning of the third act is the low point, the furthest the protagonist can possibly get from his or her goal. At the climax, the protagonist confronts the antagonist, and reconciles with the relationship character. They claim success or failure in reaching the goal. Then we have the denouement in which loose ends are wrapped up and the story reaches its conclusion.

Movie examples:

The Dark Knight, Spiderman, Titanic

The Dark Knight: Batman is the protagonist. He wants to retire and not be needed in Gotham, and ultimately, he gives up on his goal.

Spiderman: Spiderman is the protagonist. He wants to save the world by having a life of purpose and being more than the altered, small, wimpy, nerdy Peter Parker.

Titanic: Jack (Leonardo DiCaprio) is the protagonist. His is a life that could change forever after his chance meeting with Rose and his desire to have a better life. His underdog character is much-loved.

In *The Dark Knight*, the Joker is the relationship character. "Don't pretend you're like them. You're not like them, even if you'd want to be. You're a freak. Like me!" The reconciliation occurs when Batman answers the Joker's question. "Do you know how I got these scars?" "No, but I know how you got these." He tells a joke and accepts his role as the Dark Knight.

In *Spiderman*, Mary Jane is the relationship character. Peter Parker's love for her is only further complicated by her first kiss with Spiderman, making his alter ego a semi-antagonist.

In *Titanic*, Rose is the relationship character. Her life is torn between first class and steerage, between a pre-determined path and her newfound love. The boat sinking tears the audience apart in this tale of unrequited love.

In *The Dark Knight*, Harvey Dent is the antagonist. He impedes Batman by succumbing to the easy decisions and generally failing to be the white knight. Gotham needs him, and Batman wants him to be a hero, but it does not happen. Then he becomes Two-Face.

In *Spiderman*, Joe Jonas, the newspaper editor, is the antagonist. He chases front page headlines by making Spiderman the villain, further frustrating the hero's journey.

In *Titanic*, the well-dressed, first class fiancé is the antagonist. He will stop at nothing to prevent Jack and

Rose from bringing their fairytale to life. He is such a terrible character, it is easy to hate him and make Jack the hero.

Billions of dollars of in movie ticket sales tell us this formula works.

What about dramatic movies and stories?

Without drama and conflict, there is no story. A story where everyone gets along and nothing unpleasant happens will bore everyone. This is the reason for the "Rule of Drama."

Can we tell a story that is dramatic enough? Here are some ideas for this type of story:

- Children starving
- Plane crashes
- Divorce
- Dropping out of college
- Teenage pregnancy
- Alcoholism
- Mid-life crisis

And in comedy?

There are many ways to be funny, but any story we tell has to pass "the law of funny": it should only be funny in the moment. Because the surprise, the twist, the unusual behavior or the consequence of an otherwise normal action makes it funny.

We have to be careful, though, because what we think is humorous, might not be. We need to test.

Comedians test a joke or a routine many times before delivering in front of a paid audience. The practice makes it look spontaneous and natural, but professionals know every laugh took a lot of practice to earn.

Inspire me

When Sir Edmund Hillary reached the top of Mt. Everest, he was doing it for the fun of it.

"I think I climb mountains because I get a great deal of enjoyment out of it. I never attempt to analyze these things too thoroughly. But I think that all mountaineers do get a great deal of satisfaction out of overcoming some challenge. If they think it is very difficult for them, or which perhaps may be a little dangerous, then all the better."

His words, as well as his actions, have inspired everyone who has learned of his accomplishments. I am sure he hoped to have inspired people to do things for its sheer enjoyment, not to battle, or to conquer and win.

Whenever someone achieves something that could be considered impossible, it is inspirational. When we see success after incredible challenges requiring enormous amounts of preparation and dedication, we are inspired. When we imagine how hard it was to achieve, we are inspired.

If we want people to take action and change, an inspirational story works

Human beings have achieved so many impossible things: flying, driving, walking. They have an ability to inspire us through their actions. Knowing the consequences when they take a risk and challenge themselves personally and professionally makes the achievements all the more amazing.

"Inspiration" in the dictionary means the process of being mentally stimulated to do or feel something, especially something creative.

So inspiration means we now want to do something. A fire has been lit inside of us and we are action-oriented. We want to act. We feel something new, and we have a goal right in front of us.

For everyone, the goal is different. But inspirational stories exist to give that motivating force for change.

What are some inspirational stories?

Mick Fanning fights off a shark attack in a surfing competition. A few months later, he comes back to win a competition. He defies his near-death experience and fear and returns to dominate the sport he loves.

Liesel Jones from Australia wins silver in the 100-meter breaststroke at the 2008 Olympics. Her disappointment fires her up to train for four years and come back to win gold by more than a body length. And she does this in the second fastest time ever (she held the world record).

Nick Vujicic, after being born with no arms and legs, now travels the world. He inspires people with disabilities, or disadvantages, or who lacks motivation to find a purpose and meaning in life. Every day he proves we can overcome anything. Life without limits.

In our own life, we have inspirational stories. We only have to dig them out and turn them into something we can share with the audience.

We do not have to climb Mt. Everest to be inspiring. We do not have to find the cure for cancer.

When we want to tell our own stories, we have to be analytical. This means looking at the events in our life and choosing ones that we have learned from. Next, we analyze them and get the behind-the-scenes story. We learn the background and include it. We get the key moment or defining action clear in our minds. Then we outline the lesson or the moment of inspiration and how it applies to us today, and how it applies to our audience.

If we want to get ideas for inspirational stories, we can go to the TED talks online at Ted.com. Every day around the world, people go on stage to share their most passionate thoughts. They get up for pre-timed slots of between three and eighteen minutes and present their beliefs and values. They stand up and share inventions. They give us fresh inspiration to go out and live our lives.

The best thing TED did was to provide a platform for simple and inspirational ideas. Concepts that could be shared quickly. This stage allowed people who had one good idea to share it in eighteen minutes or less.

For the first time, we had the perfect environment to listen to scientists and researchers. We could learn amazing information without having to attend university or a science conference.

We can get the nuts and bolts success secrets of millionaires and billionaires. We can learn about finding love and overcoming obstacles. We can see people with disabilities and hear their stories of finding their place in the world. We can discover the facts and figures about our world. We can learn from people we may never have never seen before and be grateful.

We can all learn from this format. We could all watch at least two or three TED talks a week and learn many lessons.

Every inspirational story offers an insight into humans' amazing potential.

What about physical achievements?

From climbing Mt. Everest, to free diving 50 meters under water, from riding bicycles across Asia and paragliding the Grand Canyon, the human body, when stretched to its limits, can achieve amazing things.

People riding wheelchairs in Olympic marathons.
Amputees with prosthetic carbon fiber limbs running 100 meter sprints almost as fast as able-bodied.
Blind people doing triathlons.

Every time we hear a story that inspires us, it makes one more impossible thing possible. An inspirational story makes something unbelievable, believable.

And an inspirational leader sets an example for everyone else to follow. We like to quote leaders in our stories and to make a point, because the leader has the instant respect and trust of the audience. Now we just have to make the link between the story and our message.

Who are some inspirational political leaders?

Martin Luther King
Margaret Thatcher
Ronald Reagan
Abraham Lincoln
Indira Ghandi
Nelson Mandela
Suing Yong Ki
Justin Trudeau
John F. Kennedy

Every one of these leaders has a story we can tell and retell to help make our point.

Who else do we know that is inspirational?

How about … any creator or inventor.

Here is a small list of people that who creatively invented something to solve problems. They made life easier and more interesting for everyone.

- The Wright Brothers - a flying airplane
- Joseph Niece - first photo taken by a camera
- Percy Spencer - microwave oven
- Melitta Bentz - 1908 coffee machine
- Steve Jobs - iPhone
- Cares Crosby - the backless brassiere
- Bill Gates - Windows operating system for PC
- Edwin Land - sunglasses with a polarizing (darkening) filter
- Alexander Fleming - penicillin
- Stephanie Kwolek - Kevlar

We can tell their stories about how they worked on solving the problem. How they tried and failed. How they succeeded. How it affected their family. How their inventions changed the world.

Every invention has a different emotional meaning, depending on the audience. This is why most of the time we use universal stories that everyone can relate to.

This is why the stories of Galileo, Edison, Jobs and others are retold so many times.

Everyone is a part of the universe.

We all use electricity.

And everyone has or knows about the smart phone or iPhone.

But the professional speaker researches his audience and chooses stories that will be important and relevant.

Inspiring stories will stimulate the most important values and principles most important to the people in the audience.

Want to inspire someone to climb a mountain? Tell Sir Edmund Hillarys' story. Be the first to do something, and you are forever immortalized in history of what your achievement is.

Need the audience to consider something brave and daring? How about getting a teenager to sail around the world? Jessica Watson in her pink Ella Bache yacht has a story to tell about the perils of doing it all by yourself. And of sailing into Sydney Harbor to be met by hundreds of thousands of young people who've just found out that anything is possible.

Stories of endurance and fitness and fair play? How about playing consecutive games of football without injury or suspension? Jim Stynes played 244 consecutive games of Australian Rules football before he broke his hand and had to take a break. That was more than eleven seasons of football, and is a record that has lasted nearly twenty years, and may last forever.

Want to tell the a story of someone coming in and dominating a sport?

Swimming

The most decorated Olympian of all time, Michael Phelps, holds a total of twenty-two medals in three Olympics before Rio. He also holds the all-time records for Olympic gold medals (18—double the second highest record holders), Olympic gold medals in individual events (11), and Olympic gold medals in individual events for a male (13).

And he came out of retirement and qualified for the Rio Olympics twelve years after his first appearance in Athens in 2004. What else is possible for a record-breaker and the greatest Olympian of all time?

He's proven he was a superman, winning more (three) gold medals and qualifying in every final he swam in.

Car racing

Michael Schumacher is a retired German race car driver. He is a seven-time Formula One World Champion and is widely regarded as one of the greatest Formula One drivers of all time. He was twice named Laureus World Sportsman of the Year and he won two titles with Benetton in 1994 and 1995 before moving to Ferrari, where he drove for eleven years. His time with Ferrari yielded five consecutive titles between 2000 and 2004.

His domination of the sport was has been matched only by the fear and respect his fellow drivers have paid him. He left the sport inspiring a new generation of drivers.

Flying a plane

Earhart was the first female aviator to fly solo across the Atlantic Ocean. For this record, she received the U.S. Distinguished Flying Cross. She set many other records and wrote best-selling books about her flying experiences. She was instrumental in the formation of the Ninety-Nines, an organization for female pilots. In 1935, Earhart joined the faculty of the Purdue University aviation department, and she was a visiting faculty member counseling women on careers. She also helped inspire others with her love for aviation. She was also a member of the National Woman's Party, and an early supporter of the Equal Rights Amendment.

If she can take on a challenge like flying across the notorious Atlantic and succeed, anything is possible. For women, and for men. Who are we to say there are things that cannot be done?

Inspirational stories trigger the right emotions to help our audience remember what our message was about.

Secret #6

Before and After

These are the stories of personal transformation and they are interesting to everyone, because they put themselves into the story from the "before." When they are "in" the story, they want the "after," too. This makes it easier to lead them to follow the advice or suggestions, and the story and our teaching or training will all link together and make sense.

People want to change, but they find it easier to do so if someone else has already done it. Because they have been told it is hard to change, and people do not like it. Following the example of someone else proves to them it is possible.

The truth is, people change every day. It is just easier if they can do what someone else has done, knowing it is safe and okay.

What are some before and after stories we can tell from our own life or from the lives of others?

- Losing weight
- Learning a skill
- Making money
- Building a business

- Having a baby
- Becoming a parent
- Having a teenager
- Traveling the world
- Learning a language
- Being an employee
- Being a boss
- Working in the government
- Working in non-profit companies
- Attending a workshop
- Leading a workshop
- Developing a skill
- Teaching that skill.

When we are young, it is hard to imagine what life will be like in the future. We have a particular experience, and we view life through it. We also have no reality beyond our actual experience, which means everything that happens to us is new and a surprise.

But when we deliberately act toward a goal or a new discovery, things change. We can see where we are and where we want to be. We can see what we know and what we do not know. We can see the level we have achieved and aspire to something more.

Let us look at some of the before and after stories we can create.

Losing weight

"Before, I used to weigh two hundred seventy pounds. After six weeks, I am down to two hundred and twenty and I have fifty pounds to go. My mind was never fully committed until after I'd gotten 'Doctor Skinny's' advice.

But none of it would have been possible without the support of my friends and the great diet I've been on."

"Before, I could never get rid of the last three pounds of fat around my thighs. After just ninety days using the Ab-Blaster, I have a six-pack. My legs are lean and strong, and I am getting compliments like when I was an eighteen-year-old at university."

"Before, I had to stop at every flight of stairs to take a breath. I was puffing like a steam train. The extra thirty pounds I carried around was like a bag of bricks I couldn't shake off. After six weeks with a personal trainer, I lost ten pounds and I can see the light at the end of the tunnel. Ten flights of stairs? Bring it on!"

Energy levels

"Before I started this product, I'd need a Red Bull or an espresso at three in the afternoon at work just to stay awake. But after swapping my breakfast routine from sweet cereals to my super-shake, I have the energy to go all day without a single latte! More energy, and I am saving money, too!"

"The exercise I did as a personal trainer tired me out more than it energized me. Before, I would spend twenty sessions in group fitness training and couldn't wait to get to Friday for a long sleep. After shifting my diet according to the 'XYZ diet,' I was able to perform my fitness sessions and improve my personal best time for running five miles."

"I have always wanted to cut down the amount of coffee I drink. Two cups in the morning, and then three more lattes throughout the day. Before 'SuperCoffee,' I was spending over thirteen dollars a day, had problems with my digestion and no longer felt the kick of caffeine. After just a month on SuperCoffee, I have more energy, need less coffee, and my food is tasting delicious again!"

Skincare

"Before, I used to look in the mirror and see age lines like my grandmother. And I am only thirty-one! After just seven days of using this product, I am seeing the lines fade, and my skin is feeling soft and looking radiant."

"Before, I would see the sunspots on my skin and wonder if they would ever go away, or if they'd just get worse. After twenty-one days of using this product, the spots are gone, and my head no longer looks like a freckled teenager's. I feel like I look my age again."

Parenting and relationships

"Before, when parenting my teenager, I was at my wit's end. After I read this amazing 'Super Parent' book, I felt in control again. I have strategies for being a successful parent and enjoying having a teenager for the first time. Now, we both have a closer relationship than ever before."

"Before, my children were treating me like a stranger. After this weekend retreat, I feel I can make them my friends again."

"Before, I thought I had to be strong in our marriage and never admit to any fears or weaknesses. After listening to my husband tell me his faith in me, I feel confident enough to share with him so we can be stronger together."

"Before the baby was born, I was afraid I would be a bad parent. After the first three months, I've realized I am just a natural. I love this baby more than anything, and I know I am doing the best job I can."

Business success

"Before I read this book, I thought I was a failure and would never make things work. After learning that most people have a few businesses crash before their big success, I am moving ahead faster in the direction of my entrepreneurial dreams."

"Before, I used to have two hundred products and I worked in my business twelve hours a day just maintaining stock and getting things out on time. After we simplified our product range to three core items and four variations, sales went up, profits up, and the morale around the company went up."

"Before, I thought I had to do it all myself. After hiring my first virtual assistant, I got another and another. Now my business is ten times bigger and my overhead is smaller than it was when I rented my office in the suburbs."

"Before, I could not type more than ten words per minute. I used to look at the keys and use only two or three fingers. And I had to keep looking up at the screen. After taking the Typing Tutorial course, I've have gotten my speed up to twenty words per minute. Now, I never look at my fingers and I can finally start writing the book I always dreamed I would write."

Traveling

"Before I left home, my biggest adventure had been the annual Melbourne Show. After flying to Cambodia, I have now seen Siem Reap and the amazing history of a ruined city that was once the center of the Asian world."

"Before I went to the UK, I thought everyone was the same in England. After seeing London, Edinburgh, and Dublin, I feel I know the roots of our culture with Irish, Scottish, and English people and their unique differences."

"Before I went to Turkey, I only ever ate a kebab in my hometown. After, when I ate in Taksim Square, I had the feeling of eating authentic Turkish food in the center of the city of Istanbul, and it was the real deal."

The journey of transformation

The journey to success is never a straight road.

There are many learning experiences along the way to having a successful business. It does not matter if it is a franchise, a hairdressing salon, network marketing, or running a charity. The journey to success has a lot of detours.

If we write a story about change or transformation, it should have elements of the hero's journey. Just sharing about "being successful" is not compelling listening.

Headlines for this sort of story could be something like:

- "Secrets of the multi-millionaires: One woman's journey from the western suburbs of Sydney to a harborside mansion."
- "Building an Empire: The rags to riches fairytale of Miami's private education innovator."
- "Silicon Valley Superstar: The Oakland to Pacific Heights transition of a multimedia icon, how it all began."

People want to know how they can make it to the top too.

When people are hungry for success secrets, they love to hear other people's stories to copy or model their own journey on.

Some more headlines?

- How I lost one million dollars, and then made two million in the next six months.

- My relationship disasters, and how I created my ideal partner.

- Divorced and broke one year, married and rich the next.

- How ignoring one money-management principle crippled my two hundred thousand dollar income.

- Why hiring staff is important; HR disasters from the vault.

- Making money is easy; keeping it is hard. What I lost by not learning accounting in the first five years of my business.

- Seven sales mistakes people make every day, and why it is costing you tens of thousands of dollars in lost deals.

- Where to find your next success after your current failure.

- The path to disaster includes doing these three lazy money management activities.

What failure to success stories could we create about from our own life?

- For our final high school exams, we sacrificed partying; we studied hard and then got all "A's."

- We did not get into our chosen college or university, but did end up getting into something even better.

- We had tragic break-ups and our hearts were in pieces, until we found our true love.

- We want to be great parents and not make the same mistakes we observed growing up. How we correct these in our own parenting to feel satisfied in that role.

- We lose our job, but win the girl.

- Having stage fright and being terrified, then turning into an inspirational speaker in front of a thousand people.
- Performance anxiety when playing music in an exam, that changes to a standing ovation from the examination board.
- Being fired from a job, then getting an overseas opportunity for something that pays twice as much.
- Not getting through an acting audition, but getting a dancing job instead.
- Having a script rejected by a publishing house, then self-publishing for millions.
- Being cut from the football team, then becoming a great coach.
- Getting cut from the shortlist at drama class, then going out and attending one hundred auditions and appearing in a Hollywood blockbuster two years later.
- Not doing our homework, dropping out of school, then creating a business that made millions.

These are just for starters.

What else do we have happen in our adult life that we would call a "failure" or a "disaster"?

- Our first big relationship breakup that taught us lessons we put into a book that became a bestseller.
- Wasting money at our place of work, only to be appointed the CFO and making the business the most efficient, ever.
- Booking something non-refundable like a hotel or flight on the wrong day, only to receive an upgrade from the hotel at check-in

- Yelling at a co-worker, then becoming a trainer in equality, tolerance, and anti-discrimination.
- Physically assaulting someone, then spending time in jail, only to exit and inspire others to a life of tolerance and calm.
- Breaking our own bones at the beginning of the final year of high school, then healing and going on to win the 100-meters at the state titles.

The possibilities for stories of pain, suffering, loss, and fairness followed by their redemption, are endless.

Redemption

Maybe we have a story that talks about loss.

How we lost our job because we could not get along with our co-worker, and in a fit of rage, we punched them in the nose. We were charged by the police with assault and had a our day in court in front of the judge, where we had to be penitent, humble, and apologetic.

And despite all of that, we still received a fine, a suspended sentence, and had to make a verbal apology in front of strangers, the media, and the victim. Plus, we lost our job.

The story cannot stop there because the audience is unsatisfied.

Where is the redemption?

This must be in the second part of the story, since the audience will be waiting for it. We have to provide for their need for resolution and have the silver lining to the cloud.

After the court decision, what happened?

- Did we do community service and develop a passion for cleaning up the neighborhood?
- Did we start a home-based business to pay off the fine?
- Did we travel around and have to speak in schools about workplace violence, and then discovered we enjoyed the speaking?
- Were we so motivated to stay out of prison, we took anger management classes?
- Maybe we had an light bulb moment and moved on to the path of education in prisons to assist with people who have anger issues.
- Or we might have written a book about ways to deal with our temper.
- Or taught others how to channel our energy into other, more productive areas like sport, exercise, and our job.

We must show the silver lining in our story. There needs to be a something positive that so people can say: "Even when a bad thing happens, something good can come from it."

If we do this, people will lean forward and want to hear this story, and our next one.

Secret #7

Sales Stories

People tell me this is the best part.

Standing in the glaring spotlight in front of more than two thousand people, I had to make a good first impression. So I said the two most powerful words you can use in front of any audience, other than their names.

"Thank you."

"Thank you for the introduction. Thank you for having me here at the convention. Thank you for attending my trainings and workshops in the last twelve months. In fact, your company makes up more than thirty percent of all of our event registrations.

"Thank you for attending my personal leadership workshops. For those who have not seen it, people tell me the best part of the workshop is my goal-setting strategy. It's called the 300% shift, and it's the most powerful goal-setting concept I have ever shared.

"So I decided to record it. It's about twenty minutes long, only ten dollars, and I have just a thousand copies with me today. We will probably sell out.

"I have a few other items at our sales booth, so please come and visit.

"Thank you again for having me, and enjoy your morning tea break."

I walked off the stage, went out to our sales booth—twenty-four feet of tables covered in products to sell—and the crowd was already eight-people deep, all crowding the tables, throwing money to be the first to get the products. We sold out of all one thousand CDs in fifteen minutes, and the best part? That day we sold over $67,000 in products, our biggest day ever.

Now, this is a true story. A story I have told hundreds of times to show the power of using the words "thank you" in a presentation or a speech. It has helped me prove to people we need to tell a story in our presentation to help us sell more.

It is also proof people buy what I have to sell.

And proof people act when I say something I have prepared well.

But people do not have to believe me. If they have not met me before, then I am a stranger. But they only need to listen to the story, and it does the convincing for me.

When we sell anything, we are looking for an exchange of value. We want money for the product or service we are selling. And the best way to sell anything is to tell stories about other people who like what we have to sell.

The power of a story here is so strong, no other technique even comes close. We can talk all day long about our product, but people do not trust us. They trust the reality of our customers.

Testimonials
Endorsements
Recommendation

All these give our prospect more reasons to buy from us.

If this is true, then we should cut our presentation. Change it from so much talking about our product's facts and figures, to telling and showing more stories of people using the product. Have them share what they love about it. Show videos of them using the product. Written reviews and references add weight and legitimacy to our claims and to our stories.

What to do first

We need to get the stories from our customers.

It can be as simple as asking for feedback, then sharing that feedback with our future customers. It might be a review on our website or Facebook page, then we can screenshot it, print it, share it, and/or include it in our formal marketing and promotions material. Maybe it is a video testimonial gathered at one of our live sales presentations. When people are expressing positive emotions, they give the best reviews.

How do we get the feedback?

- Put a survey on our website.
- Send an email asking for feedback.
- Talk to customers immediately after a sale.
- Make a video when someone has been using a product for a week or a month.
- Get the written endorsement or review of a book when people get an advance copy.
- Have a feedback form available in our store for instant feedback.
- Copy hotels who use a form beside the bed to ask "How did we do?" Make it easy to give feedback.

- Follow up with a call or message a few days after a sale.
- Build the expectation of feedback or a review by asking for it early in the sales process.
- Get referrals to other friends every time we make a sale. And in that referral, ask what part of the product or service they think their friends would be most interested in.

At Art Jonak's Mastermind event, attendees are interviewed on camera after keynote speeches. The energy level is high, and the people speaking are natural and positive about the experience.

At Anthony Robbins' UPW weekends, people walk on fire and then post about it online for days and weeks afterwards. This is the best advertising: When the customer has a transformational experience and spontaneously shares it.

When we have someone in our store, we can encourage them to take photographs with the product they have bought. They can pose with staff and the photos in the store itself provide free marketing, possibly viewed by hundreds or thousands of prospective customers. This can be done with just the time it takes to help people do what they would do anyway.

Strategy is important in building a good referral and recommendation loyalty program. Just giving something small as a bonus helps the customer feel good about helping us.

If we have a retail store, photos and videos on the internet will be great advertising for us and the happiest customer is the one who just bought. This is the time to get their photo, and their referral.

Don't have a store? Maybe we sell something else or offer another service?

What stories will our customers tell?

- How they got a product that helped them lose weight
- How their skin looks younger by applying the magic cream
- How they see the chance of making additional income
- Where they can now travel because of the extra income they received from their own sales
- How they were inspired by a speech
- How they saved money
- What their goals are
- Which of their goals have now been achieved since working with us
- How coaching them for success has changed their life
- When they are going to retire
- Who they feel has made an impact on their life
- The books they are now inspired to read
- The relationships they have created in their personal and professional life

Stories help salespeople sell, without the pressure.

Stories give real examples of what other customers have experienced.

Stories use the power of the third party.

A third party is someone external to the salesperson and the customer. Someone who is objective. A third party has power because of their anonymity and they have no agenda when talking to the prospect or audience.

There is no better marketing tool. We can use a third party in front of an audience. If they are present, they can stand up and tell their story.

How can we use this?

If the third party had a great results in making money with a business, then they can use the before and after story secret.

First share how much money they had when they started.

Second tell how they felt and how hard they worked.

Finally, how they now feel about having financial success.

If they lost weight using a diet or fitness method?

They can talk about the weight they used to be, using their arms to show "how big," or show their old pair of pants, or photographs up on the big screen. When they share it, the emotional state in the present is powerful.

We can tell their stories in the form of testimonials and references, in writing and from the stage. From that moment forward.

We might read a success story off a card or a website.

We might read out an email sent in to us.

We can put their quotes on banners and up on slides.

We can use the testimonials as our opening story.

We can borrow their successful result until we have our own.

We can edify them and say what a great job they did.

We just need to memorize and share these stories with the energy and passion they deserve. After all, these are often the stories of a changed life. And that is worth being passionate about.

Conclusion

Secret Stories - "Curiosity and irresistibility"

Funny Stories - "Telling it with humor and making it memorable"

Past and Present Stories - "When I was Young"

Me and You - "Personal stories and the stories of others"

Emotional Stories - "Create an emotional response"

Before and After - "Transformation"

Sales Stories - "Testimonials, referrals, reviews, and the power of the third party"

These seven types of stories will give us different directions in which to take our talk. When we need particular reactions or engagement, we can use the appropriate story.

Some stories can be short, almost like quotes—one or two sentences, or a paragraph. Some stories are can be long and tell life lessons, running for five to ten minutes.

We can do this on a conference call, in a sales presentation, or at a training. We can use stories online and offline. We can use them in the beginning, the middle, and the end of our presentations. All we have to do is fill our talk with interesting stories that engage our listeners.

Never stop telling stories. Stories are the description of our lives.

More Secrets

There are a few free resources you can take advantage of to be more confident speaking.

Be sure to subscribe to the Public Speaking tips at the authors website, www.markdavis.com.au.

Take advantage of Mark's other books on Public Speaking at www.amazon.com/author/markdavisaustralia

Join the Public Speaking Mastermind group in Facebook. www.facebook.com/groups/publicspeakingmastermind.

Mark is also also available for speaking at conferences and conventions, as well as doing webinars, calls, and private coaching.

For anything else, please email mark@markdavis.com.au or contact him via +61-404-178-126.

www.ingramcontent.com/pod-product-compliance
Lightning Source LLC
Chambersburg PA
CBHW071821200526
45169CB00018B/576